Christmas Coloring Book
For Adults

Nina.M

Christmas Coloring For Relaxation Meditation

Copyright: Published in the United States by Nina.M
Published November 2017

All rights reserved. No part of this publication may be reproduced, stored in retrieval system, copied in any form or by any means, electronic, mechanical, photocopying, recording or otherwise transmitted without written permission from the publisher. Please do not participate in or encourage piracy of this material in any way. You must not circulate this book in any format Nina.M does not control or direct users' actions and is not responsible for the information or content shared, harm and/or actions of the book readers.

ISBN-13: 978-1979511216

ISBN-10: 1979511217

www.ingramcontent.com/pod-product-compliance
Lightning Source LLC
Chambersburg PA
CBHW082220220526
45470CB00010B/3245